CZERNY

OPUS 821
FOR THE PIANO

160 EIGHT-MEASURE EXERCISES
(Short Studies)

Maurice Hinson, Editor

This edition is dedicated to Mrs. Frances Gibson with admiration and appreciation.

Maurice Hinson

Foreword

Carl Czerny was born in Vienna on February 20, 1791. After early instruction by his pianist father, he appeared in public as a child prodigy in 1800. Subsequently he became a student of Beethoven and by the age of 15, he had established himself as a respected piano teacher. Among his artist pupils were Theodor Döhler, Sigismond Thalberg, Theodor Kullak, Alfred Jaëll and Franz Liszt. His nonetude works comprise over 300 graduals and offertories, as well as symphonies, masses, writings in music history and theoretical treatises; his opus numbers are near the one-thousand figure. Czerny's one planned international concert tour was cancelled because of the Napoleonic Wars. He died in Vienna on July 15, 1857.

Czerny's talent was remarkable: within a narrow harmonic scheme he developed a prodigious understanding of finger movements possible on the keyboard. He composed many volumes of studies that feature rapid, feathery, well-articulated passages, mainly for the right hand. His style was smooth, pretty and ear-tickling when played fast; he was very popular during his lifetime.

Czerny taught piano for 10–12 hours a day; his genius for teaching was so cultivated that he could quickly devise the correct study for a student who exhibited any particular area of weakness. His performances were considered fluid and brilliant and he gave the Vienna premiere of Beethoven's Piano Concerto No. 5 ("Emperor") in 1811.

Czerny recommended that each of the Op. 821 eight-measure exercises be practiced at least eight times in succession. The exercises include scalar figurations, contrast of legato and staccato, trills, arpeggios, solid and broken octaves, grace notes, full chords, turns, quick alternation of hands, double-note thirds and sixths, fast repeated notes, transposition, ornaments, wide skips, hand-crossings and contrary motion playing. Their brevity, attractive melodies and figurations make them most appealing. They are written for the intermediate to advanced student.

Third Edition
Copyright © 2003 by Alfred Music
All rights reserved. Produced in USA.

Cover art: The Old Burgtheater in Vienna, *1783*
by *Carl Schütz (Austrian, 1745–1800)*
Colored etching
Historisches Museum Stadt Wien, Vienna, Austria
Erich Lessing/Art Resource, New York

160 Eight-Measure Exercises
Short Studies

Practice each number at least 8 times in succession, thereby creating one large study.

Carl Czerny
Op. 821

4

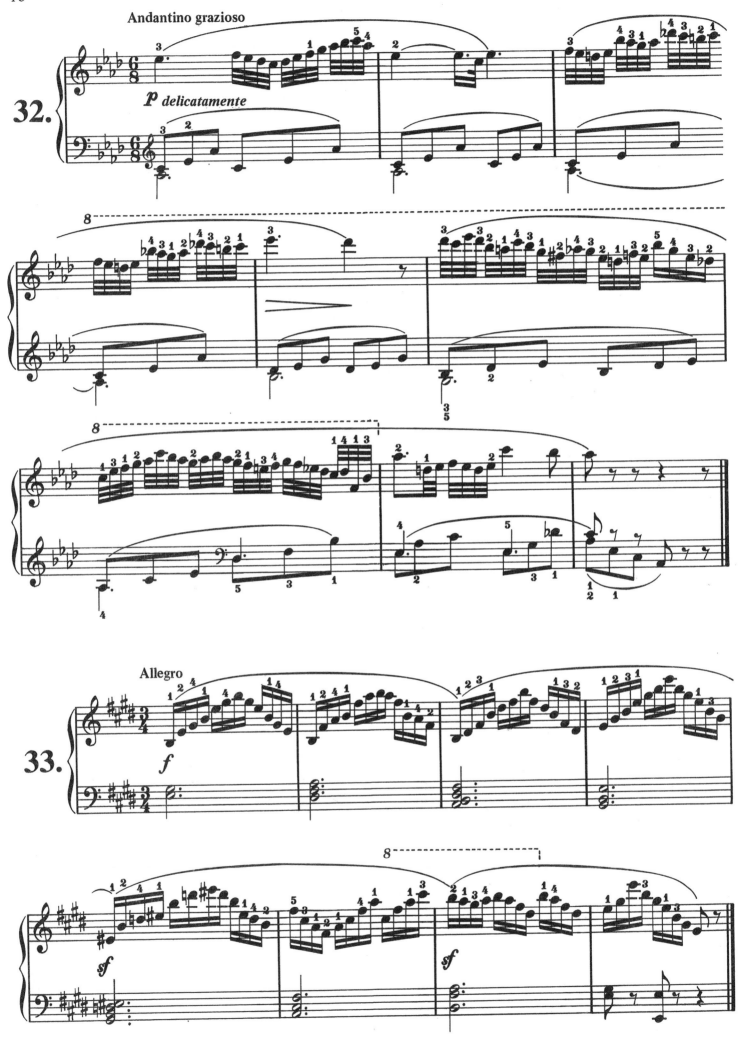

40.

41.

26

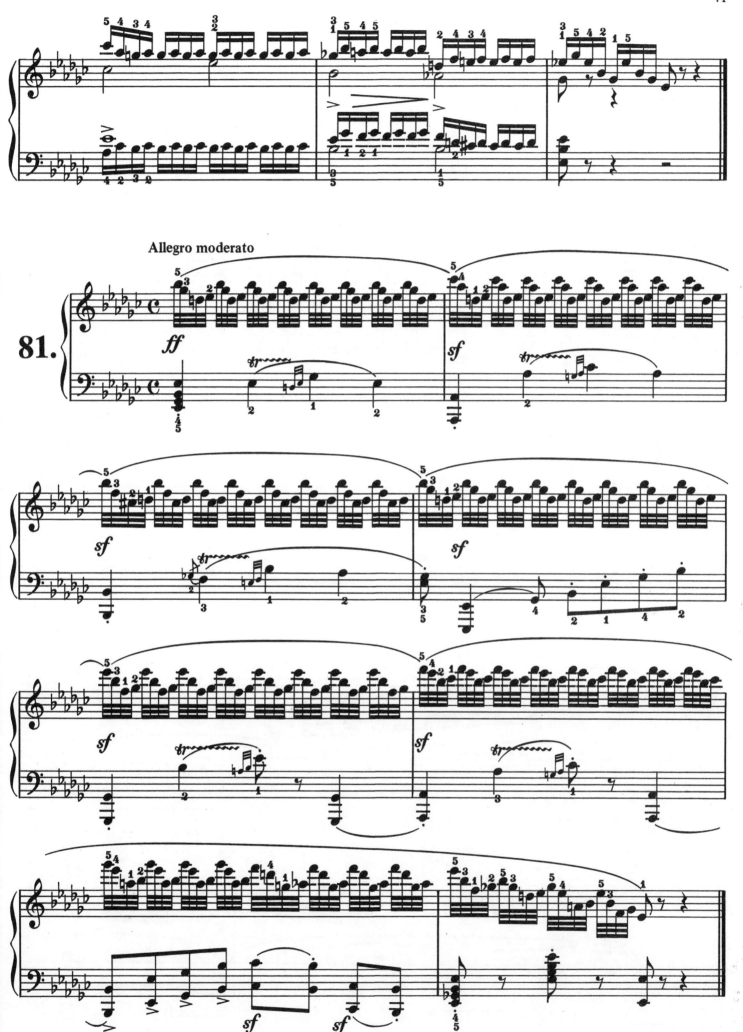

Allegro moderato

81.

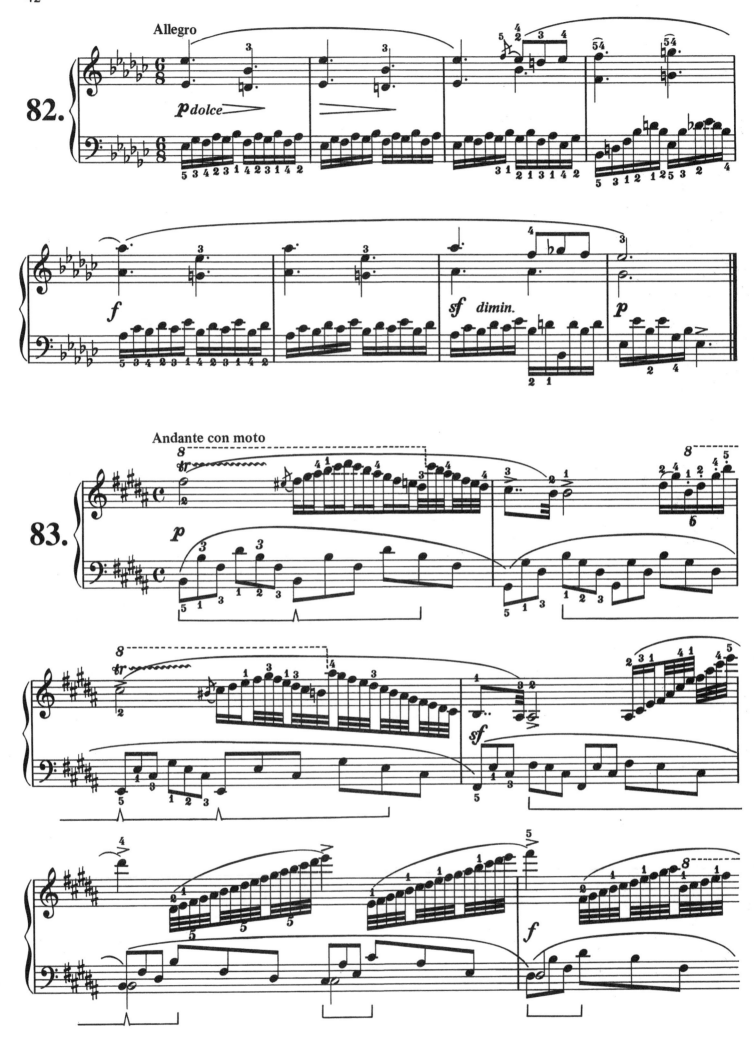

44

Allegro

90.

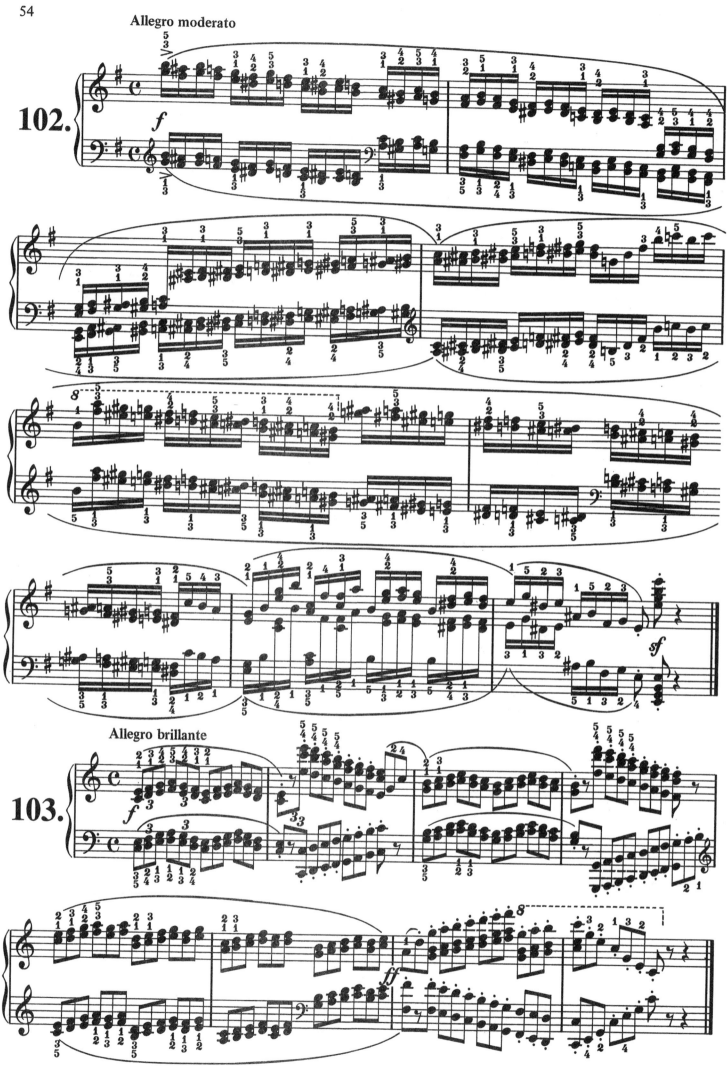

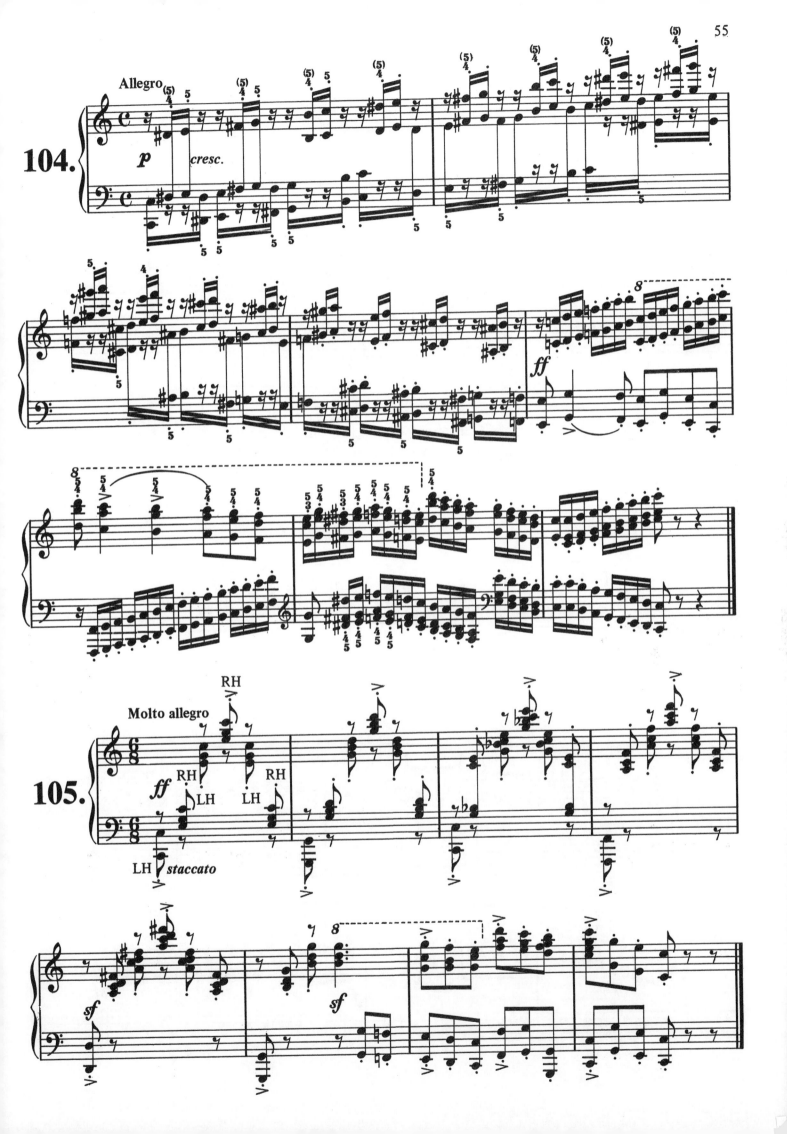

56

Allegro moderato

110.

Vivace

111.

ⓐ Also transpose one-half step higher.

112.

113.

ⓒ Also practice in F♯ minor.

123. Andante

124. Allegro con fuoco

ⓐ Also transpose one-half step higher.

125. Allegro vivace

ⓐ *ff*

126. Allegro

f

127. Allegro

ten. *mf* *ten.* *cresc.*

f

ⓐ Also transpose one-half step higher.

ⓐ Also transpose one-half step lower.

131. Allegretto moderato

@Also transpose one-half step lower.

138.

139.

ⓐ Also transpose one-half step lower.

74

75

76

ⓐⓑⓒ Also transpose one-half step higher.

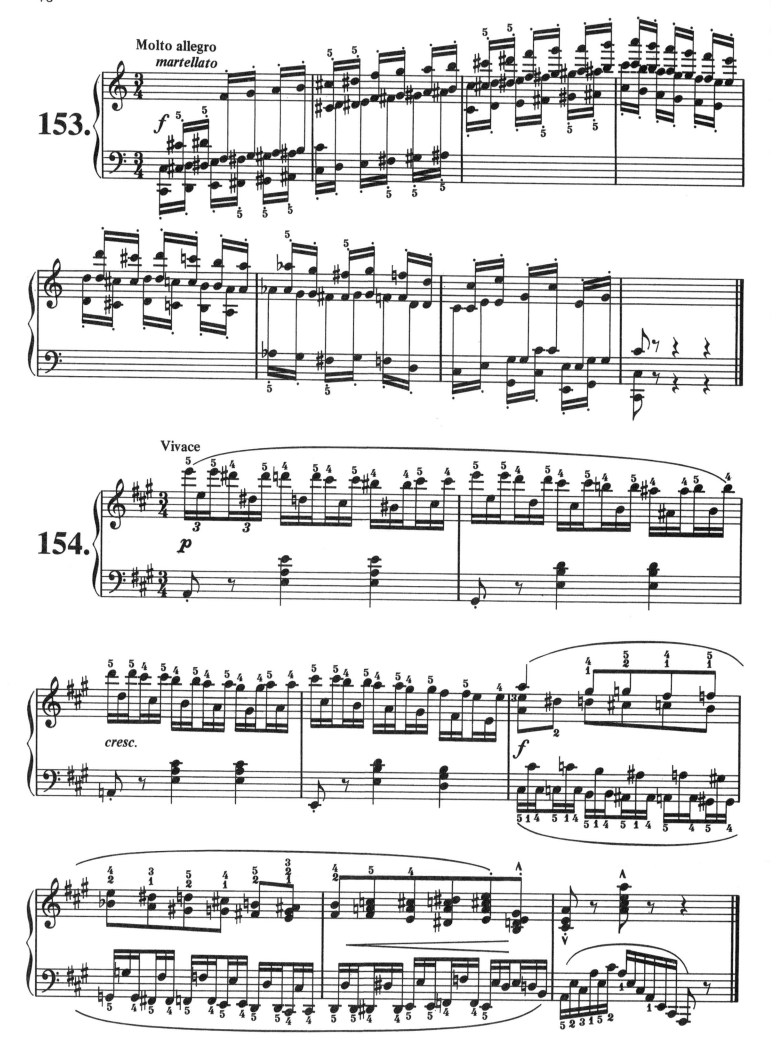

155.

156.

157.

Allegro vivace

158.

Allegro

81